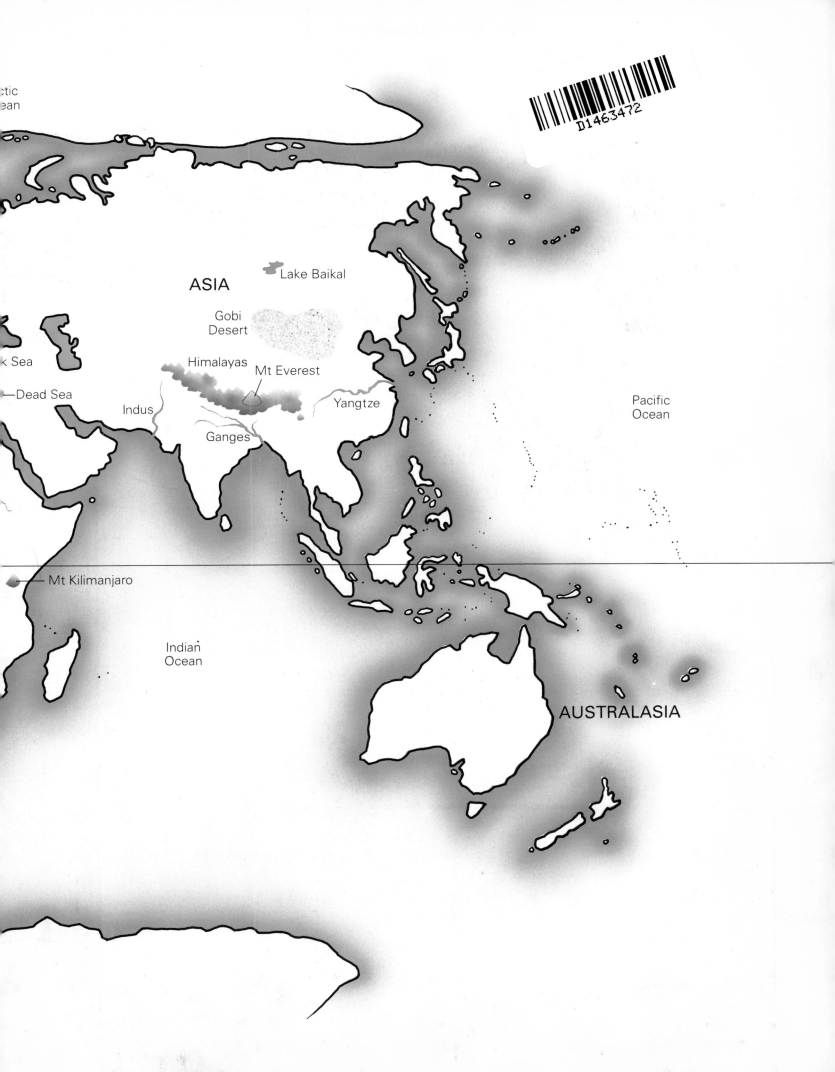

ctic
ean

ASIA

Lake Baikal

Gobi
Desert

Himalayas
Mt Everest

k Sea

Dead Sea

Yangtze

Indus

Pacific
Ocean

Ganges

Mt Kilimanjaro

Indian
Ocean

AUSTRALASIA

Edited by Debbie Lines
Designed by Brigitte Willgoss

Map illustrations by Oxford Illustrators Limited

Brimax Books would like to thank
the following companies for the loan
of their transparencies:

Chris Fairclough Colour Library:– pages: 22BL; 38A; 39A; 42A.

The Photo Source:– pages: 40A; 20B; 42BR; 43A; 44B,

Picturepoint-London:– pages: 6A; 8AL; 8AR; 8B; 9A; 9BL; 9BR; 10AR; 10B;
11B; 12B; 13A; 13B; 14A; 14B; 16AL; 16B; 17R; 17BL; 18AL; 18BL; 19AR;
22AR; 22BR; 23AL; 23AR; 23B; 24BL; 24BR; 25BL; 25BR; 26A; 26B; 27AL;
30AL; 30AR; 30B; 31AL; 31R; 32BL; 33A; 33BL; 34; 35; 36A; 36B; 37AL;
37BR; 39C; 39B.

Zefa Picture Library (UK) Ltd:– front and back covers;
inside pages:– 6B; 10AL; 11AL; 11AR; 12A; 14C; 16AR; 17AL; 18AR; 18BR;
19AL; 19B; 24A; 25A; 27AR; 27BL; 27BR; 28A; 28B; 31BL; 32A; 32C; 32BR;
33BR; 37AR; 37BL; 38C; 38B; 42BL; 43BL; 43BR; 44A; 44AL; 44AR; 44B.

ISBN 0 86112 603 3
© Brimax Books Ltd 1989. All rights reserved.
Published by Brimax Books Ltd, Newmarket, England 1989.
Printed in Portugal

MY FIRST ATLAS

Written by Pamela Mayo

Brimax Books · Newmarket · England

North America

The United States of America and Canada together form the very rich continent of North America.

The north of the continent stretches a third of the way around the Arctic Circle. Much of the land here is permanently frozen and the sea can sometimes freeze in winter.

In the south of the continent it is a great deal warmer and there are desert lands in Arizona and Nevada. In the very south, it is so warm that the sea in the Gulf of Mexico is heated up. The water is warm as it flows past Florida on its way across the Atlantic Ocean to Europe. Hurricanes are a constant threat in this area.

High mountains called the Rockies run down the west side of North America, from the cold Arctic Ocean down to the warm south where the United States of America meets Mexico. On the eastern side of the continent is a smaller range of mountains – the Appalachians.

Between these mountain chains are great grassy plains with enormous cattle ranches, rolling fields of wheat and other crops.

North America is rich in minerals like gold, silver, coal and iron. Oil has also been found in Alaska, Texas and the Gulf of Mexico.

▲
Huskies (Alaska, USA)
Much of Alaska is covered by snow all year round. Dogs called huskies used to pull people on wooden sleds over ice and snow. Now snowmobiles are becoming popular.

▲
The **Interstate Road** crosses the Rocky Mountains in the USA. The road follows the Colorado River before the river plunges through the largest gorge in the world – the Grand Canyon.

ARCTIC OCEAN

GREENLAND
(DENMARK)

ICELAND

ALASKA
USA

Godthab

CANADA

Ottawa

UNITED STATES
OF
AMERICA

Washington

Bermuda

MEXICO

GULF OF
MEXICO

North America has people from many different lands. First there were the American Indians and the Inuit. Then came people from many countries of Europe, Asia and Africa. Between them they make North America a land of varied cultures and traditions.

▲

Fisherman (Greenland) This fisherman is mending his net. Fishing here is very important. Not much can be grown in Greenland because it is covered in ice and snow for most of the year.

▲

Pipeline (Alaska, USA) There are large oil fields in Alaska. Large pipes carry the oil from the fields to the coast. There is an oil pipeline right across Alaska from north to south.

Niagara Falls (Canada) ▶
One part of the Niagara Falls is in Canada, the other is in the USA. These Falls are the Canadian part. Little boats can take visitors up the gorge below the Falls.

▲
Quebec (Canada) The St. Lawrence River flows from the Great Lakes to the Atlantic Ocean. The Canadian city of Quebec is near the mouth of the river. The French-looking castle is a hotel.

▲
Banff (Canada) Many visitors come to Banff National Park in the Rocky Mountains. It is one of Canada's oldest and most famous parks. Beyond the lake lies an icy glacier.

▲
The **Grizzly Bear** lives in the Rocky Mountains of North America. It is the biggest of the bears. This bear is hunting for fish. Bears can be dangerous if you make them angry.

▲

Navajo Indian
(Arizona, USA) This
Navajo Indian woman is
weaving coloured wools
into a rug to sell to tourists.

▲

Monument Valley (Arizona, USA) Strange
shapes looking like castles and tall buildings rise
out of the broad flat lands of Monument Valley.
There are few towns in Arizona, so roads can go
for miles in a straight line across the land.

Disneyland
(California, USA)
This huge amusement park
was opened in 1955
and millions of people have
visited it over the years. It is
a city of magic palaces and
fantastic rides where you
can meet your favourite
characters from Walt
Disney's cartoons
and films.

▶

Las Vegas (Nevada, USA) is famous for the gambling in the many casinos there. People go there hoping to win money. The bright lights invite people to see shows, as well as to gamble.

Football (USA) American football is a popular sport in the USA. It is a more dangerous game than European football. The players wear strong helmets and shoulder pads for safety.

Rodeos are popular events to go to. Cowboys show how they can ride bareback on a horse, stay sitting on a bull or on a wild horse, and 'rope' or lasso calves from horseback.

Mount Rushmore (South Dakota, USA) The faces of four American presidents have been carved into a cliff in the Black Hills, South Dakota. They are George Washington, Thomas Jefferson, Abraham Lincoln and Theodore Roosevelt.

The White House (Washington D.C., USA) ▶

The President of the United States of America lives in the White House in Washington D.C. It has over 100 rooms. The most famous is the Oval Office. Washington D.C. is named after the first American President, George Washington.

▲
**Wheat Harvesting
(Canada/USA)** The wheat fields on the plains of Canada and USA stretch for miles. They are so large that it takes several combine harvesters to cut and thresh the wheat.

◄ **Central Park
(New York, USA)**
Central Park is one of the few green spots on Manhattan Island. All around it are New York's skyscrapers. In winter, people go to the park for ice-skating.

Central and South America

▲
Rio de Janeiro (Brazil)
Modern skyscrapers stand tall in Rio de Janeiro. The old customs house below was built by the Portuguese, as Brazil was under Portuguese rule for several hundred years.

The lands of Central and South America stretch from Mexico in the north, through the hot lands around the equator, to cold lands in the south near the Antarctic.

There are thick rain forests with valuable timber. The great plains have cattle. The river basins have rubber, cocoa and bananas. Coffee is grown on the hillsides of the mountains. The Andes Mountains stretch all the way down one side of South and Central America.

There is also the driest desert in the world. Rain did not fall in the Atacama Desert in Chile for over 400 years.

The Amazon is the world's greatest river. It carries more water to the sea than any other river.

There are many minerals in South America but some are difficult to mine because many parts of the continent are hard to get to. Some parts are still unexplored.

A narrow piece of land connects South America to Central America. The Panama Canal has been cut through so that ships can get from the Atlantic to the Pacific Ocean.

U.S.A.

Bermuda
(UK)

ATLANTIC
OCEAN

MEXICO

Gulf of
Mexico

Mexico
City

Belmopan

CUBA

Nassau

BAHAMAS

HAITI

DOMINICAN REPUBLIC

Havana

Santo Domingo

GUATEMALA

JAMAICA

BELIZE

Kingston

PUERTO RICO

Guatemala

Pt. Au Prince

San
Juan

Guadeloupe (France)

Martinique (France)

San Salvador

HONDURAS

NICARAGUA

Caribbean
Sea

BARBADOS

EL SALVADOR

Managua

TRINIDAD &
TOBAGO

Tegucigalpa

COSTA RICA

Caracas

VENEZUELA

Pt. of Spain

GUYANA

San José

Panama

Georgetown
Paramaribo

FRENCH GUIANA

Cocos Island
(Costa Rica)

PANAMA

Bogota

Cayenne

COLUMBIA

SURINAM

ECUADOR

Quito

PERU

BRAZIL

Lima

**Tierra del Fuego
(Argentina)**

Argentina stretches from
hot lands in the middle of
the continent to very cold
lands in the south. At its
southern tip there are icy
lakes and rivers, and snowy
mountains where it is
windy, wet and cold.

Brasilia

La Paz

BOLIVIA

PARAGUAY

Asunción

Lake Titicaca (Peru)
The boatman steers
his boat among the
reeds of the highest
lake in the world. It is
Lake Titicaca, the
largest freshwater
lake in South
America. The lake is
used for shipping and
fishing.

CHILE

Santiago

Beunos Aires

URUGUAY

Montevideo

ARGENTINA

Falkland
Islands
(UK)

South Georgia
(UK)

Central and South America were conquered by people from Spain and Portugal many years ago. Many Indian tribes live in these parts but the cities look Spanish. Spanish is spoken everywhere except Brazil where Portuguese is spoken.

▲ **Sugar Cane (Mexico)** Sugar is grown in many hot countries. These Mexicans are cutting down the tall canes by hand. The canes are then chopped up in machines. At the sugar-mills the sweet juice is squeezed out.

▲ **St. Lucia (West Indies)** The fish have been collected with large nets. The boats have been pulled up under the coconut palms. The afternoon sun shines down on the beautiful fishing harbour of St. Lucia.

Lake Maracaibo (Venezuela) Some of the largest oil fields in the world are in and around Lake Maracaibo. This is not a proper lake because it enters the sea. The cranes in the picture are called derricks and they show where the oil is being drilled. ▶

◀ Angel Falls (Venezuela)

The Angel Falls are the tallest waterfalls in the world. They drop 3212 feet (979 metres). Until about fifty years ago, when a pilot called Jimmy Angel crashed near them, only the local Indians knew about them.

▲ Bananas (Central America)

For many people in hot countries bananas are an important food. This is because they can be sold to people in the colder countries of Europe and North America where bananas cannot be grown.

◀ Yanomani Indians

(Venezuela) Very few people live in the jungles of Venezuela. Most people live by the coast. The Yanomani Indians live deep in the forests, eating the animals they can catch.

▲
Manaus (Brazil) Large ships can travel about 800 miles (1200km) up the Amazon River to Manaus in the centre of Brazil. Beyond Manaus, smaller boats can travel a further 800 miles (1200km) or so into Peru.

▲
Indians (Brazil) Many different kinds of people live in Brazil. Some are descended from Europeans and Africans. But the poeple who were there first were the Indians. This Indian family is making baskets to sell.

▲
**Carnival
(Rio de Janeiro, Brazil)**
People dress in beautiful costumes and dance in the streets for this festival.

▲
Machu Picchu (Peru) The Spanish conquered the Inca people over 450 years ago, but their city at Machu Picchu was not found until 1911. The Incas built temples, palaces, canals, and roads that linked a large kingdom in the Andes Mountains.

▲
Uru Fisherman (Lake Titicaca, Peru) and their families live on floating islands made of reeds. They also use the reeds to make their houses and their boats.

▲
Gaucho and Sheep (Chile) South American cowboys are called gauchos. As well as sheep, cattle are important for food in this part of Chile.

▲
La Paz (Bolivia) is very high up in the Andes mountains. It has steep cobbled streets and busy markets. As well as fruit, the Indians bring vegetables like maize and potatoes to sell.

19

Europe

Europe is a small but wealthy continent, and is made up of many countries. Some are large, like Russia. Others are small, like Luxembourg. In nearly every country a different language is spoken, but some languages, like French, Italian and Spanish have some very similar words.

Some of the northern countries of Europe are close to the Arctic Ocean and North Pole and have very cold winters when the sea can sometimes freeze over. Southern Europe, around the Mediterranean Sea, has quite mild winters, sometimes with no snow at all.

There are no deserts in Europe, as it does not get hot enough. But there are parts of Northern Europe, close to the Arctic Circle, where the ground is frozen and no trees can grow. This area is called tundra.

The highest mountains are the Alps, in Switzerland, but they are a great deal lower than the Himalayas of Tibet, in Asia.

Europe has many industries that vary from country to country and for most of Europe, the fairly mild climate means that many different crops can be grown and livestock raised.

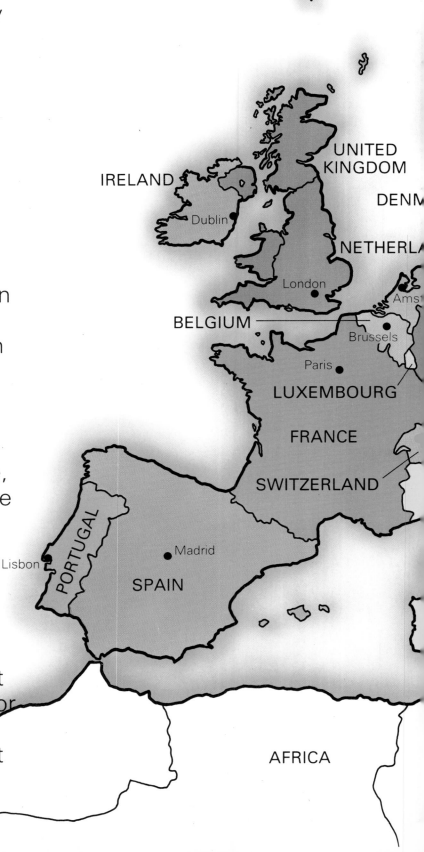

NORWAY

SWEDEN

FINLAND

Oslo

Stockholm

Helsinki

Copenhagen

EAST
GERMANY

Berlin

Warsaw

POLAND

Prague

CZECHOSLOVAKIA

EST
MANY

Vienna

AUSTRIA

Budapest

HUNGARY

ROMANIA

Belgrade

Bucharest

YUGOSLAVIA

BULGARIA

Sofia

ALBANIA

Rome

Tirane

Athens

GREECE

MALTA

CYPRUS

MEDITERRANEAN SEA

MOSCOW

UNION
OF
SOVIET
SOCIALIST
REPUBLICS

ASIA

CASPIAN
SEA

BLACK SEA

Even though languages are very different from country to country, travelling around Europe is quite easy. No country is difficult to get to.

Fishing Trawler (Wick, Scotland) ▶
These fishermen are making their way home from the sea around the north of Scotland. They have had a good day's fishing. The seagulls fight for the bits thrown overboard, as the fishermen clean their fish.

Big Ben (London, England)
Big Ben is the most famous clock in the world. It is part of the British Parliament Buildings. It is visited by thousands of tourists each year, who will travel in the famous red double decker buses and black taxis.
▼

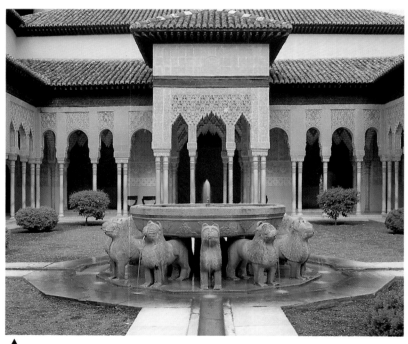

▲
Alhambra (Spain) This beautiful palace was built over 800 years ago by the Moors, who invaded Spain from Africa. It overlooks the city of Granada in Southern Spain.

◀ The Eiffel Tower (Paris, France)

lights up the night sky. You can see almost all of Paris from the top. It was built in 1889 for the Great Exhibition and is just over 975 ft (300 metres) tall.

▲

The Camargue (France)

This area by the Mediterranean Sea is famous for its flat, marshy land and wild horses. This very popular game of bowls is played in all parts of France and is known as boule or petanque. It is played with metal balls.

◀ Brussels (Belgium)

The Grande Place in Brussels is visited by many tourists who go to see the wonderful flower displays. Brussels is famous both for its flower markets and its beautiful old buildings.

▲

Neuschwanstein Castle (West Germany) Long ago, in Germany, rich Barons and Princes built castles overlooking lakes and rivers. The tall towers would be used as look-outs to spot enemy soldiers.

▲

Windmills (Holland) The Dutch farmers use windmills to pump salt water off the land into the canals. Nowadays they sometimes use pump-engines instead.

▲

Motor Show (Turin, Italy) Many people come to see the latest cars at the annual International Motor Show. You can see cars from many countries, some for the very first time.

◄ **Grand Canal (Venice, Italy)** In Venice, there are no roads for cars. Instead, people travel in boats and gondolas along the many canals that go through the city.

▲

Athens (Greece) A guard in Greek costume watches over the Tomb of the Unknown Soldier in Athens.

▲

Varna (Bulgaria)
The Black Sea is an inland sea and Varna is where many people of Bulgaria go for their holidays. Varna has very warm summers but very cold winters.

Lenin Shipyard (Gdansk, Poland)

Many fine ships are built in this shipyard in Gdansk, one of the most important Polish ports on the Baltic Sea. Gdansk has a natural harbour where ships collect and deliver cargoes of coal, iron, cereal and timber.

Kremlin (Moscow, Russia) Moscow, like many great cities, was built on a river. It is the capital of Russia. The government buildings are behind the walls of an ancient fort, and together are called the Kremlin.

St. Basil's Cathedral (Moscow, Russia)

This fairy-tale building is, in fact, a church. It is near the Red Square where large parades of thousands of Russian soldiers are held.

Lapp (Finland)

In this part of Finland roads would be of no use in the deep snow. Instead the Lapps use reindeer to pull their wooden sleighs.

Viking Museum (Oslo, Norway)

The Vikings were brave sailors and great explorers from Norway. The Viking Museum shows an old longship, the Oseberg. The Vikings used it to go on 'raids', for slaves and treasure.

Timber (Norway)

There are many fir trees in Norway. Their wood is used for making houses, furniture and paper. The timber is floated down the rivers to be sent to other towns and countries.

Asia

Asia is the biggest continent in the world and it also has the largest population. It stretches from the very cold lands near the North Pole, to the hottest lands near the Equator and from lands by the Mediterranean Sea to the islands on the Pacific Ocean.

Asia is a land of opposites. There are very high, cold lands in Tibet where you can find Mount Everest, the world's highest mountain. There is also the lowest land, around the Dead Sea. There are great deserts such as the Gobi Desert, and plains such as the Mongolian Steppes where very few people live. But there are also great cities in China, Japan and South East Asia where millions of people live. Most people work on the land — there are a lot of people to feed.

There is enormous wealth here in oil, in the Middle East, and industries in Japan and Hong Kong. But also, some of the poorest people live in Asia.

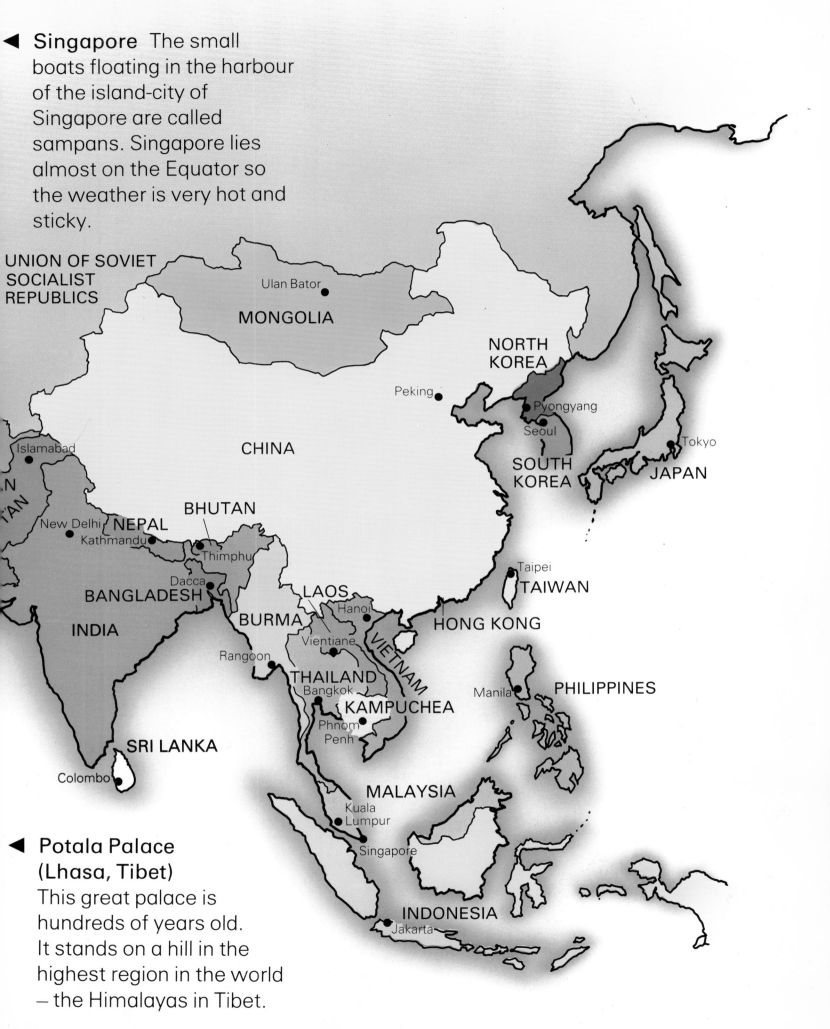

◄ Singapore The small boats floating in the harbour of the island-city of Singapore are called sampans. Singapore lies almost on the Equator so the weather is very hot and sticky.

UNION OF SOVIET
SOCIALIST
REPUBLICS

MONGOLIA

Ulan Bator

NORTH
KOREA

Peking

Pyongyang

Seoul

CHINA

SOUTH
KOREA

JAPAN

Tokyo

Islamabad

New Delhi NEPAL BHUTAN

Kathmandu

Thimphu

Dacca

BANGLADESH

INDIA

BURMA

LAOS

Hanoi

Vientiane

Taipei

TAIWAN

HONG KONG

VIETNAM

Rangoon

THAILAND

Bangkok

KAMPUCHEA

Manila

PHILIPPINES

Phnom
Penh

SRI LANKA

Colombo

MALAYSIA

Kuala
Lumpur

Singapore

**◄ Potala Palace
(Lhasa, Tibet)**
This great palace is hundreds of years old. It stands on a hill in the highest region in the world – the Himalayas in Tibet.

INDONESIA

Jakarta

Dress and traditions vary from country to country in Asia. Light clothes can be worn all year round in Southern Asia, whereas people in Tibet must wear warm clothes against the mountain cold.

▲

The **Taj Mahal (Agra, India)** is made of white marble and took nearly 20 years to build. It was built by an Indian Emperor as a tomb for his beloved wife.

▲

Benares (India) Indians do not wash in the River Ganges just to keep clean. It is important for Hindus to bathe here at Benares, as part of their religion.

Mount Everest (Nepal) ▶
Every mountaineer hopes to climb the world's highest peak, Mount Everest, which is just over 5 miles (8km) high. But it is a dangerous mountain to climb because the weather is very bad here for most of the year. The top was not reached until 1953.

◄ Family Scene (Nepal)
Nothing is wasted in Nepal. The cow dung drying on the wall will be used for fuel to keep family fires alight. Firewood is hard to find.

▲
Tea Picking (Sri Lanka)
This tea picker chooses the best leaves to pick. She tosses them into the bag on her back.

◄ The Great Wall (China)
is the largest building project ever. It is hundreds of miles long with a wide stone road along its top. It was built over 2000 years ago, to keep out invaders.

The **Bullet Train (Japan)** ▶
is one of the fastest trains in
the world. Behind it is
Mount Fuji. The even sides
of the mountain show that it
is a volcano.

The Golden Pavilion ▶
(Kyoto, Japan)
The Golden Pavilion is
a Buddhist temple. Its walls
are covered in real gold. It is
in a lovely garden with
ponds and waterfalls, now
covered in winter snow.

▲
Hong Kong is a tiny island off the
coast of China. It has more people for
its size than any other country in the
world.

▲
Hong Kong is a very busy place with
many factories that make goods to
sell all over the world. Streets and
shops are full of people day and night.

◀ **Floating Market (Thailand)** These boats are used as shops. You can buy all sorts of vegetables and fruits from the women at this floating market in Thailand.

▲

In **Bali (Indonesia)** rice is grown in hillside paddy fields that the farmers have to wade through to plant and look after the rice.

▲

Bali (Indonesia) Rice is the main food for most people in Asia. When it is harvested, the stalks are bundled, then the rice grains are threshed out.

Australasia and the Pacific Islands

Australia is the smallest continent but the sixth largest country in the world. Even so, few people live here in comparison to Asia. Most people live in big cities by the sea. Inland the weather is too hot and the land is too dry for crops or livestock. Where sheep and cattle can be raised, the ranches, or stations, are enormous, with many miles between neighbours. Australia has many industries – engineering, iron and steel, shipbuilding, oil refining, food processing and many more.

New Zealand is two large islands, North and South Islands. It has high, snowy mountains and some volcanoes. Sheep are very important in New Zealand for the meat and wool, and there are more sheep than people here.

There are thousands of islands in this part of the Pacific Ocean. All of them are volcanic or coral islands. Their main industry is tourism.

To the south is the Antarctic, a land permanently frozen and covered in ice. The ice is sometimes as much as 2¼ miles (4.8km) thick.

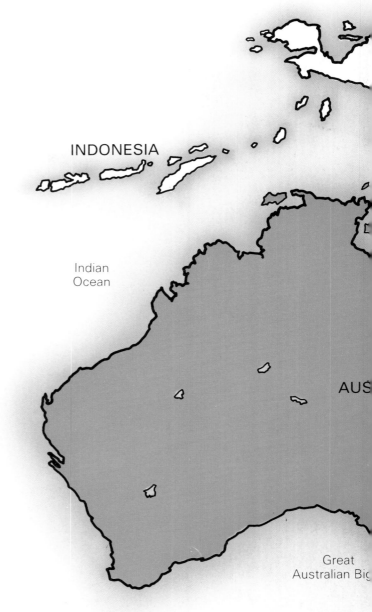

INDONESIA

Indian
Ocean

AUS

Great
Australian Big

Southe

Opera House (Sydney, Australia)

The Opera House looks rather like an old-fashioned sailing boat and was opened in 1973.

Mt Ngauruhoe (New Zealand)

The smoke and steam coming from the top of this volcano are a warning that the volcano could explode, pouring lava over the nearby land. ▶

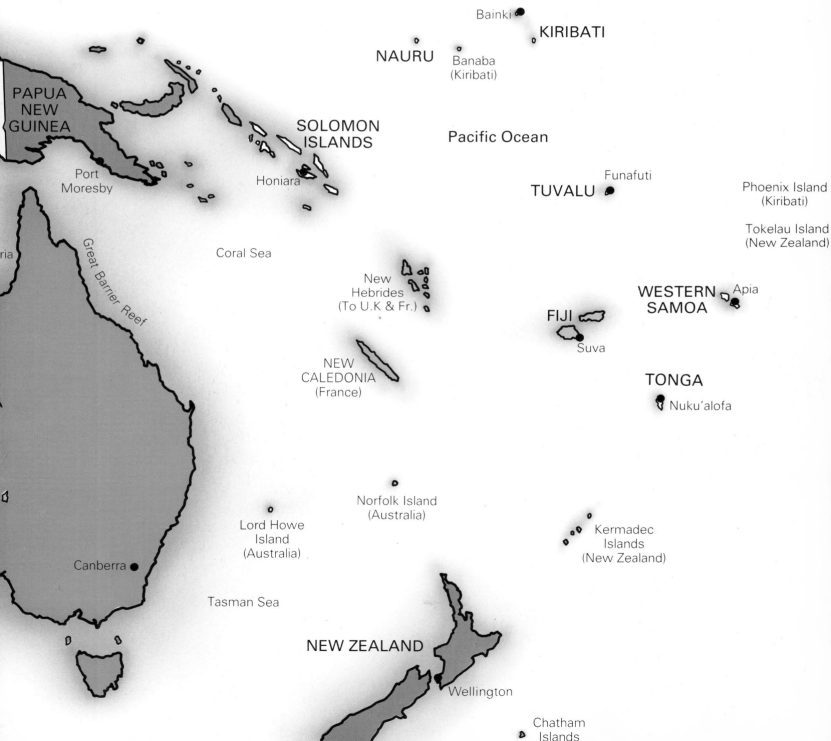

Bainki

KIRIBATI

NAURU

Banaba (Kiribati)

PAPUA NEW GUINEA

SOLOMON ISLANDS

Pacific Ocean

Port Moresby

Honiara

Funafuti

TUVALU

Phoenix Island (Kiribati)

Tokelau Island (New Zealand)

Coral Sea

ria

Great Barrier Reef

New Hebrides (To U.K & Fr.)

WESTERN SAMOA

Apia

FIJI

Suva

NEW CALEDONIA (France)

TONGA

Nuku'alofa

Norfolk Island (Australia)

Lord Howe Island (Australia)

Kermadec Islands (New Zealand)

Canberra

Tasman Sea

NEW ZEALAND

Wellington

Chatham Islands (New Zealand)

Hundreds of years ago Europeans sailed to the Pacific Ocean to trade and explore. They found the Aborigines in Australia, the Maoris in New Zealand and the Polynesians on the islands. Eventually they came to settle here.

▲
Ayers Rock (Australia) rises above the dry flat desert in central Australia. It is very old and is one of the largest blocks of stone in the world. It is an important religious place for Aborigines.

Arnheim (Australia)   ▶
Aborigines were the original inhabitants who were there when Europeans first discovered Australia. This Aborigine is painting on bark. His picture tells a story from long, long ago.

▲

Ballarat (Australia) When gold was first found in Australia in the 1850's many people went there from Europe and America hoping to get rich. Towns were abandoned if the gold ran out.

▲

Cattle Herding (Australia) Some farms in Australia are very large. Many of them have lots of cattle, so the farmers may use helicopters to round them up.

▲

Duck-billed Platypus Furry animals do not usually lay eggs, but the platypus does. When Europeans first saw this animal they thought it was made from several different animals.

▲

Koalas live in eastern Australia in eucalyptus trees. Although they look like bears they are more like kangaroos as they carry their babies in pouches.

Flying Doctor In Australia, some people live in places a long way from the towns. Doctors have to go by plane to see them if they are very sick. They are called Flying Doctors.

Barrier Reef (Australia) This is probably what the Aborigines saw when Europeans first went to Australia in their large sailing ships. All the Europeans could see were palm trees and beautiful flowers. They didn't know that it was very dry inland.

Papua New Guinea (Indonesia) Traditions are very strong in the Pacific Islands. This man is wearing his traditional dress of leaves and feathers but it does not stop him from using a fairly modern form of transport – the bicycle.

Sheep Herding (New Zealand)

There are many sheep in New Zealand. In winter their coats grow very thick. In spring their wool is cut off and sent to other countries to make clothes. The sheep are also used for meat.

Maoris (New Zealand)

The Maoris came to New Zealand from islands in the South Pacific long before Europeans arrived. They were a fierce people and this war canoe would have held many warriors.

Tonga (South Pacific)

In Tonga, you can pin money on the dancer's dress if you like her dancing.

Africa

Africa is a large, hot continent. No places get very cold, even in winter.

The Equator passes through its middle. There the sun is very hot all year round. But there is also lots of rain. Everything grows very quickly. Not many people live in these thick forests and swampy jungles.

The grasslands have many wild animals living there – elephants, lions, zebra and giraffes and many others.

There are also deserts where no rain falls. Most of North Africa is made up of the Sahara Desert. The smaller Kalahari and Namib Deserts are in the south.

In the very north and very south it rains in winter and fruits like oranges, lemons and grapes grow well.

There are high mountains, such as Mount Kilimanjaro, and large lakes. Africa also has two of the longest rivers in the world, the Nile and the Zaire.

Some of Africa's cities are many centuries old, like Cairo. Others like Johannesburg, are less than 200 years old.

Gold, diamonds and copper are important minerals which are found in Africa.

Fadiout Island (Senegal, West Africa)
Here in Senegal, grain is stored on platforms built on logs. This protects them from the water and hungry animals. The boat is made from a hollowed out treetrunk.

THE GAMBIA

Dakar
Banjul

Bissau
BISSAU
Conakry
SIERRA
LEONE
Mon

EUROPE

ASIA

MEDITERRANEAN SEA

• Rabat
• Algiers
Tunis •

MOROCCO
TUNISIA
• Tripoli

ALGERIA
LIBYA
EGYPT
Cairo •

RITANIA
ott •

MALI
NIGER
CHAD
Khartoum •
SUDAN
DJIBOUTI
Djibouti •

BURKINA
• Bamako
• Ouagadougou
Niamey •
N'Djamena •
Addis Ababa •
ETHIOPIA

EA
own •
IVORY
COAST
GHANA
BENIN
NIGERIA
CAMEROON
SOMALIA
Mogadishu •

• Abidjan
Accra •
Lomé
Porto
Novo
Lagos •
Yaounde •
CENTRAL
AFRICAN REPUBLIC
Bangui •
UGANDA
KENYA

TOGO
Malabo •
EQUITORIAL
GUINEA
CONGO
Kampala •
Nairobi •

GABON
Libreville •
RWANDA
Kigali •
Bujumbura •
BURUNDI

Brazzaville •
Kinshasa •
ZAIRE

CABINDA
TANZANIA
Dodoma •

ATLANTIC
OCEAN
Luanda •
INDIAN
OCEAN

ANGOLA
MALAWI
Lilongwe •

e Mountain
ZAMBIA
Lusaka •
MOZAMBIQUE

th Africa)
Harare •

n sailors from Europe
saw land at the
hern tip of Africa they
this flat-topped
ntain. They called it
e Mountain. The white
d is the 'tablecloth'.
w lies the city of
e Town.
ZIMBABWE
Antananarivo •

NAMIBIA
Windhoek •
BOTSWANA
Gaborone •
Pretoria •
Maputo •
Mbabane •
MADAGASCAR

SWAZILAND
LESOTHO
Maseru •
REPUBLIC OF
SOUTH
AFRICA

41

Many different tribes of people live in Africa. Most have dark skins and curly hair. Some people, such as those in the desert, move around all the time. Others live and work in towns, or they may be farmers or miners.

Dye Vats (Morocco)

The skins of goats are used to make Morocco's beautiful leather. The skins are soaked in special vats or tanks in chemicals for several months. This is called tanning. The leather is then used for hand bags, belts, purses, cases and shoes.

In **Algeria,** the camel is a very precious animal because it can go for many days without water in this dry land.

Market (Senegal, West Africa)

Market women at this town in Senegal show their vegetables. The people of Senegal can also grow maize, rice and groundnuts.

◄ Sphinx (Egypt)

The Great Sphinx has the body of a lion and the head of an ancient Egyptian King or Pharoah. It was carved thousands of years ago out of a large rocky hill. It lies close to Cairo.

▲

Masai Warriors (Tanzania)

The Masai of East Africa keep very strong and fit by drinking cow's milk and blood. This huge jump by one of the men is part of a warrior's dance.

▲

Safari (Kenya)

Today, most visitors hunt with cameras rather than guns. They see game like these elephant from the safety of a safari bus.

Mombasa (Kenya) ▶

Mombasa in Kenya has a fine beach. But it also has sea worms which burrow into the wood. This man is using palm fronds to burn them off his boat.

Kenya These beautiful ▶ trees are called Flame Trees. They grow in other parts of Africa but are best known in Kenya.

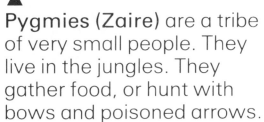

Pygmies (Zaire) are a tribe of very small people. They live in the jungles. They gather food, or hunt with bows and poisoned arrows.

Tobacco Plantations When the leaves of the tobacco plant turn from green to yellow it is time to pick them. They are then dried in barns and sold by auction. Many farmers in Zimbabwe grow tobacco.

◄ Johannesburg (South Africa) Miners in South Africa drill for gold deep under the ground. They have lamps on their safety helmets to help them see in the pits. Most of the world's gold comes from South Africa.

NORTH POLE

Arctic

Greenland

Baltic Sea

NORTH AMERICA

Lake Superior

St Lawrence

Atlantic Ocean

Alps

E

Lake Michigan

Lake Huron

Rocky Mountains

Colorado

Lake Erie

Lake Ontario

Mediterranean Sea

Appalachians

Arizona Desert

Mississippi

Pacific Ocean

Sahara Desert

Gulf of Mexico

CENTRAL AMERICA

Panama Canal

AFRICA

Lake Maracaibo

Equator

Amazon

Zaire

Lake Titicaca

SOUTH AMERICA

Namib Desert

Atacama Desert

Andes

SOUTH POLE

Antarctic